From the first song recorded in Scripture we learn that redeemed people are singing people. With biblical clarity and pastoral warmth, DeMars calls the church to lift her voice in response to God's glorious salvation. This is a timely and needed encouragement, reminding us that congregational singing is not merely tradition but a vital act of worship flowing from hearts captivated by the glory of Christ.

Matt Boswell
Pastor, The Trails Church, Celina, Texas;
Hymn writer

I've spent most of my life planning, polishing, and platforming performing artists—marketing, merchandising, and every-thing in between. For years, my world revolved around the seamless execution of performances designed to captivate an audience. But for the past decade, as a pastor, I've worked to pull apart the polish, performance, and platform mentality that has shaped so much of modern worship culture.

Sean DeMars offers a needed corrective. *Redemption Song* shifts worship from the stage to the saints, from polished performance to biblical participation, from an audience watching to a people singing. Deeply rooted in Scripture, this book reminds us that worship isn't about production—it's about proclamation. It's not about a platform, but a people. And at its core, it's biblically informed worship for an audience of One.

Thomas J. Terry
Founder, Humble Beast

A great little primer that will help ministers and the congregation. I encourage you to read it.

Jonathan Carswell
Founder, 10ofthose.com

Redemption Song is a wonderfully punchy reminder of why Christians sing. The people of God, the world over, have always been known as a "singing people". Why is that? Sean DeMars walks through the theology and practice that has typified God's people for thousands of years. From Yembiyembi, Papua New Guinea, to Rochester, New York, to the shores of the Red Sea, God's people sing, and we will sing till the King returns—and from then on—for eternity.

Brooks Buser
President, Radius International

Most people know that God's people sing. But why the church sings, what she sings, and how she sings matters too. In this short but rich book, Sean DeMars sums up the biblical why, what, and how of congregational singing. It's a valuable resource for all Christians, but especially the pastors, elders, and worship teams shaping their church's singing culture.

Brett McCracken
Senior Editor, The Gospel Coalition

Sean DeMars is a faithful pastor who has labored to help his church embrace a biblical view of worship. Now, in *Redemption Song*, he kindly gifts sound wisdom on a crucial matter to the church at large. DeMars wonderfully prods us to understand why we should sing, what we should sing, and how our services can bring the utmost glory to God. It doesn't matter how large or small your church may be, this little book is fit for every believer who cares about worship in the church—and that's every believer! The gospel is simply too good not to sing, and this book will help us all sing better. I plan to give one to each family in our church, and I'd encourage you to do the same.

Aaron Menikoff
Senior Pastor, Mount Vernon Baptist Church
Atlanta, Georgia

In recent years, we have been blessed by a reformation of the pulpit, with renewed emphasis on expository preaching, Christ-centered proclamation, and faithfulness to authorial intent. Likewise, the church has experienced a revival in biblical ecclesiology, recovering the importance of meaningful church membership, a plurality of elders leading, deacons serving, and the proper practice of church discipline. Yet, amid these vital reforms, congregational singing is often neglected—left in the shadows when it, too, stands in great need of reformation. In this excellent book, Sean DeMars directs us to God's Word, reminding us that singing is not an afterthought but an essential act of worship, designed by God for His glory and the edification of His people. *Redemption Song* will challenge, encourage, and inspire you to sing with biblical intentionality.

Josh Buice
Pastor, Pray's Mill Baptist Church, Douglasville, Georgia; Founder, G3 Ministries

A church service without congregational singing is just a concert with an extended lecture. Singing together is, perhaps, the weirdest thing Christians do in our culture of personally-curated playlists and headphones. Congregational singing testifies to our self-denying love for God and the others in the room. In *Redemption Song*, Sean Demars provides a concise, accessible reminder that broad participation in congregational singing is vitally important to the health of a local church. His reflection on the song of Moses in Exodus 15 is a useful resource to encourage Christians to drop their guard and make a joyful noise to the Lord.

Andrew Spencer
Associate Editor, The Gospel Coalition

If true worship is our response to God's revelation in Christ, then singing is not just appropriate—it's necessary. Why? Because the glory of God's redeeming grace is too great for mere speech. Yet much of today's worship music is designed for individual consumption rather than congregational singing. In Redemption Song, Sean Demars helps us recover our bearings, refocusing our hearts on singing together. Rooted in Moses's song in Exodus 15, Demars equips us to proclaim God's truth with wonder and joy. If you want to encourage your congregation to sing heartily to the Lord and to one another, buy several copies and pass them around.

Juan R. Sanchez
Senior Pastor, High Pointe Baptist Church
Austin, Texas

God delights when His people's mouths are filled with songs of praise. But He doesn't just want any song. He delights in songs that are sung with joy and faith according to His Word. *Redemption Song* is a brief and remarkably insightful booklet that helps God's people grow in singing to God as He is worthy.

Garrett Kell
Pastor, Del Ray Baptist
Alexandria, Virginia

SEAN DEMARS

REDEMPTION SONG

A PRIMER ON SINGING FOR THE PEOPLE OF GOD

CHRISTIAN
FOCUS

Unless otherwise noted, Scripture quotations are from the Holy Bible, English Standard Version, copyright © 2001 by Crossway Bibles, a publishing ministry of Good News Publishers. Used by permission. All rights reserved. ESV Text Edition: 2011.

Scripture quotations marked NIV are taken from the Holy Bible, New International Version, Copyright © 1973, 1978, 1984, 2011 by Biblica, Inc.™ Used by permission. All rights reserved worldwide.

Scripture quotations marked BSB are from The Holy Bible, Berean Standard Bible, BSB is produced in cooperation with Bible Hub, Discovery Bible, OpenBible.com, and the Berean Bible Translation Committee. This text of God's Word has been dedicated to the public domain.

Copyright © Sean DeMars 2025

print ISBN 978-1-5271-1323-7
ebook ISBN 978-1-5271-1334-3

10 9 8 7 6 5 4 3 2 1

Published in 2025
by
Christian Focus Publications Ltd,
Geanies House, Fearn, Ross-shire,
IV20 1TW, Great Britain.
www.christianfocus.com

Cover design by Rhian Muir

Printed and bound by Gutenberg, Malta

All rights reserved. No part of this publication may be reproduced, stored in a retrieval system, or transmitted, in any form, by any means, electronic, mechanical, photocopying, recording or otherwise without the prior permission of the publisher or a licence permitting restricted copying. In the U.K. such licences are issued by the Copyright Licensing Agency, 4 Battlebridge Lane, London, SE1 2HX. www.cla.co.uk

Contents

Introduction: The Artist and the Engineer 9

Insight 1: Sing 17

Insight 2: Sing in Response 27

Insight 3: Sing Together 33

Insight 4: Sing to God, about God 37

Insight 5: Sing the Truth 43

Insight 6: Sing the Whole Counsel of God 47

Insight 7: Sing History 51

Insight 8: Sing as a Leader 55

Insight 9: Sing to Bear Witness 61

Insight 10: Sing in Wonder 65

Insight 11: Sing with Joy 69

Doxology 73

Appendix:
1. The Regulative Principle 75
2. Case Studies on the Flexibility of
   the Regulative Principle 85

Recommended Reading 95

INTRODUCTION

The Artist and the Engineer

Dividing all human beings into all-or-nothing binary categories is a crude and unsophisticated way of viewing the world. People are complex, and almost no one is all one thing or another—introvert or extrovert, partier or planner, pessimist or optimist.

Nevertheless, it is sometimes helpful to lump people into categories based on their natural inclinations, giftings, and temperaments. I've found, for example, that when it comes to worship, there are basically two kinds of Christians—the artist and the engineer.

- **The artist** tends to be guided by feeling, intuition, and experience.
- **The engineer** tends to be guided by facts, logic, and reason.

Although very few people are pure artist or engineer, most of us tend to lean one way or another. (If you don't know which way you lean, ask the person who knows you best. They'll have a quick answer for you, I promise.) For better or worse, these leanings permeate every aspect of our lives, including the way we think about worship.

Over the years, I've found that many of the "engineer Christians" would be perfectly content to walk into church right before the sermon after the singing and the praying is over. These engineer Christians love a good logical sermon, laden with propositional truth claims, syllogisms, and cross references galore. Throw in a chart of some kind and the engineers will ascend to the highest heaven!

The artist Christian, on the other hand, is more than happy to sing for most of the service, but would prefer to trim the sermon down to something like a fifteen-minute devotional. The artists want to *feel* more than *think*, to *experience* more than *analyze* and *interpret*.

There's nothing wrong with being an artist or an engineer, as long as you're open to letting God's Word correct your instincts, intuitions, and inclinations where they may be out of line with God's vision for faithful corporate worship … which is what this book is all about.

THE NEED

I wasn't planning on writing a book about worship, but then I preached through the Song of Moses one

Introduction

Sunday as part of an expositional series through the book of Exodus. When I did, I found a song that offered encouragement *and* correction to both the artist and the engineer. In Exodus 15, I found a description *of* and prescription *for* corporate worship that has much to say to the modern church. In Exodus 15, we find the *Song of Moses*. But more than that, we find God. Not just any God, but the God of the Bible. And the God of the Bible is a God who reveals Himself through reason and beauty, logic and creativity, prose and poetry, propositional truth claims and musical melodies. In Exodus 15, we encounter a God who leads His people through stories, sermons, and *songs*.

The Song of Moses recounts the incredible saga of God leading His people through the perils of the Red Sea to salvation on the farther shore. But what you really have to understand about the *song* of Exodus 15 is that it comes right after the *narrative* of the same event in chapter 14, and that's on purpose. Why? Well, because narrative is not enough.

As God inspired Moses to write the Exodus story, a mere factual recounting of the salvation story was not sufficient. In recording the events of redemptive history, God didn't just want truth, He also wanted beauty. He didn't just want prose, He also wanted poetry. He didn't just want a story, He also wanted a soundtrack.

We're going to spend the rest of our time in this little book taking a closer look at the Song of Moses, but my aim is not to study the *content* of the song. There are many fantastic books and commentaries that you can consult on the particulars of the crossing of the Red Sea. In this book I'd like us to step back and consider what this song has to teach us about corporate worship more broadly. But before we dive in, allow me to get ahead of a potential objection.

Some of you may be wondering what a song from several thousand years ago, written in the desert, under the Old Covenant, can possibly teach us about modern corporate worship. Well, as it turns out ... quite a lot, actually.

The fundamental pattern of worship has not changed since the days of Moses, because the same God who led Israel to worship Him by the sea is the same God who leads us to worship Him in the church, and the nature and character of our God never changes (James 1:17). The basic pattern of biblical worship is the same from the beginning of Genesis to the end of Revelation. Some of the details may change along the way, but the broad contours are the same from the beginning of the story to the end. I think you'll see what I mean by the time you finish reading.

As we work through the Song of Moses together, I want to invite you to consider eleven insights that should give shape to the way we worship as the body of Christ. Some of these insights may seem obvious to you. Great, you've been discipled well! But even when an insight seems obvious to you, I'd still like you to consider it as carefully as if it were a fresh revelation. After all, we rarely know things as well as we think we do, and we usually need to be reminded as much as we need to be initiated. Or, as the Apostle Paul put it in his letter to the Philippians,

> To write the same things to you is no trouble to me and is safe for you. (Phil. 3:1)

Finally, some of these insights may challenge or even frustrate you. Your initial gut-reaction may be to argue or disagree, which you're certainly free to do! But I want to gently challenge you, dear reader, right here at the outset of the book, to try and read with an *open* mind and a *humble* heart. If you're anything like me, I'm sure you wouldn't say that you've got this worship thing figured out. Right? But we're always striving to grow in faithfulness! So, if you can agree, at least in theory, that you don't worship God perfectly (yet!), then allow yourself to be stretched and challenged by some of the more difficult portions of this little book. And always ask yourself, "Does this line up with the Word of God?" If it doesn't, discard it immediately. But if it does, receive it with joy (Acts 17:11).

Now, with all that in mind, I'm going to ask you to do something that may seem strange at first, even though it shouldn't. Would you take a moment, before reading any further, to pause and pray? To ask God to guard you from error and lead you into truth? Ask God to encourage you where you need to be encouraged, and correct you where you need to be corrected?

* * *

Okay, now let's read the text:

> Then Moses and the people of Israel sang this song to the LORD, saying,
>
> "I will sing to the LORD, for he has triumphed gloriously;
>   the horse and his rider he has thrown into the sea.
> The LORD is my strength and my song,
>   and he has become my salvation;
> this is my God, and I will praise him,
>   my father's God, and I will exalt him.
> The LORD is a man of war;
>   the LORD is his name.
>
> "Pharaoh's chariots and his host he cast into the sea,
>   and his chosen officers were sunk in the Red Sea.
> The floods covered them;
>   they went down into the depths like a stone.
> Your right hand, O LORD, glorious in power,
>   your right hand, O LORD, shatters the enemy.
> In the greatness of your majesty you overthrow your adversaries;

you send out your fury; it consumes them like
stubble.
At the blast of your nostrils the waters piled up;
  the floods stood up in a heap;
  the deeps congealed in the heart of the sea.
The enemy said, 'I will pursue, I will overtake,
  I will divide the spoil, my desire shall have its fill
  of them.
  I will draw my sword; my hand shall destroy
  them.'
You blew with your wind; the sea covered them;
  they sank like lead in the mighty waters.

"Who is like you, O Lord, among the gods?
  Who is like you, majestic in holiness,
  awesome in glorious deeds, doing wonders?
You stretched out your right hand;
  the earth swallowed them.

"You have led in your steadfast love the people
whom you have redeemed;
  you have guided them by your strength to your
  holy abode.
The peoples have heard; they tremble;
  pangs have seized the inhabitants of Philistia.
Now are the chiefs of Edom dismayed;
  trembling seizes the leaders of Moab;
  all the inhabitants of Canaan have melted away.
Terror and dread fall upon them;
  because of the greatness of your arm, they are
  still as a stone,
till your people, O Lord, pass by,
  till the people pass by whom you have purchased.
You will bring them in and plant them on your own
mountain,
  the place, O Lord, which you have made for

> your abode,
> the sanctuary, O Lord, which your hands have
> established.
> The Lord will reign forever and ever."

For when the horses of Pharaoh with his chariots and his horsemen went into the sea, the Lord brought back the waters of the sea upon them, but the people of Israel walked on dry ground in the midst of the sea. Then Miriam the prophetess, the sister of Aaron, took a tambourine in her hand, and all the women went out after her with tambourines and dancing. And Miriam sang to them:

"Sing to the Lord, for he has triumphed gloriously; the horse and his rider he has thrown into the sea."

(Exod. 15:1-21)

INSIGHT 1

Sing

The first thing that I'd like to show you is that God's people sing.

This seems self-evidently true when you come to a text where God's people are, well … singing. But you'd be surprised how many times over the years I've had to persuade fellow Christians that it is not only their *duty* to sing, but also their *privilege*. So let me say this as clearly and as simply as possible: The entire Bible bears witness to the truth that the people of God are a singing people.

Why do God's people sing? Well, for several reasons. First of all, God's people sing because we are created in the image of a singing God. Listen to Zephaniah 3:17:

> The LORD your God is in your midst,
>   a mighty one who will save;
> he will rejoice over you with gladness;

> he will quiet you by his love;
> he will exult over you with **loud singing**.

So, one reason why we sing is because we, the children of God, love to imitate our heavenly Father.

> Therefore be imitators of God, as beloved children. (Eph. 5:1)

Children who love their parents imitate them. As Christians, the Holy Spirit has enabled us to love our heavenly Father, and now our greatest hope is to be like Him in every way (1 John 3:2). And so we sing.

Another reason why we sing is because God commands us to. Consider what Paul writes to the churches at Ephesus and Colossae:

> And do not get drunk with wine, for that is debauchery, but be filled with the Spirit, **addressing one another in psalms and hymns and spiritual songs, singing and making melody to the Lord with your heart,** giving thanks always and for everything to God the Father in the name of our Lord Jesus Christ, submitting to one another out of reverence for Christ. (Eph. 5:18-21)

> Let the word of Christ richly dwell within you **as you teach and admonish one another with all wisdom, and as you sing psalms, hymns, and spiritual songs** with gratitude in your hearts to God. (Col. 3:16 BSB)

Or consider the psalmist:

> Let us enter His presence with thanksgiving;
> let us make **a joyful noise** to Him in song.
> (Ps. 95:2 BSB)

So it's pretty clear that singing our worship to God is not optional. It's a command that must be obeyed by all who claim to love God.

> If you love me, you will keep my commandments.
> (John 14:15)

Now, if you're like most people, you probably want to know the *why* behind the command to sing. "Okay," you might say, "I get it. God commands His people to sing. But why does He command His people to sing? What's the purpose?" The answer (at least in part), is simple: because singing is good for our souls.

While the aspirations of the transhumanist project seem nearer now than ever before, the fact of the matter is that human beings are not computers. We don't communicate in binary code. We don't have a circuit board or an operating system. We are more than mere circuitry. Humans have a mind, will, and emotions, and we communicate and comprehend best when every aspect of our being is fully engaged, and few things have the ability to engage the whole person like the act of singing.

Singing engages …

- the intellect
- the imagination
- the memory.

Let's consider each in turn.

You know, without me having to explain very much at all, how well singing engages the **memory**. Think about how often you find yourself singing a hymn for the rest of the day after church, or how you wake up in the middle of the night with a song stuck in your head. There's something about beauty and melody and rhythm that makes information stick. This is why we put the ABCs into song form. The song makes it stick.

Have you ever forgotten the words to *Jesus Loves Me, This I Know*?

> Jesus loves me, this I know,
> for the Bible tells me so.
> Little ones to him belong;
> they are weak, but he is strong.
>
> Yes, Jesus loves me! Yes, Jesus loves me!
> Yes, Jesus loves me! The Bible tells me so.

Bible studies are great, sermons are powerful, and Scripture memorization always strengthens the soul, but singing the gospel helps us remember it in a way that listening to it and meditating on it alone can't.

When you read through the Bible, you find that the great problem of God's people is that they are constantly forgetting His grace. I call it gospel amnesia. So God, in His loving kindness, is constantly arranging their lives together to help them remember their great salvation. From the holy days of the Old Testament liturgical calendar to the celebration of the Lord's Supper "in remembrance" in the New, God is constantly helping His people do what they need to do so that they don't forget their great salvation. One of the main ways that God makes the gospel stick in our hearts is by commanding and inviting us to sing it together with one voice, heart, and mind (Rom. 15:6).

Second, singing engages the **intellect**. The best hymns don't just move our hearts, they also teach our minds. Consider the lyrics of this children's song that, Luke, our music leader, has turned into a hymn for our local church:

> God made the earth and filled it full
> With seas and trees and animals
> And then He made a man
> But Adam, he was incomplete
> So God gave him a helper, Eve
> To carry out His plan
>
> This happy husband and his wife
> They showed the world what God is like
> Until they disobeyed
> And even though they lost it all
> We still see fingerprints of God
> In everyone He makes

We are the image of the God of all the world
He made us boys (boys)
He made us girls (girls)
Different pieces of the puzzle
Joined together perfectly
We are just the way God wanted us to be

Again, consider a more familiar hymn, *Christ, the True and Better*:

Christ, the true and better Adam
Son of God and Son of man
Who when tempted in the garden
Never yielded never sinned
He who makes the many righteous
Brings us back to life again
Dying, He reversed the curse, then
Rising, crushed the serpent's head.

Christ, the true and better Isaac
Humble son of sacrifice
Who would climb the fearful mountain
There to offer up his life
Laid with faith upon the altar
Father's joy and only son
There salvation was provided
Oh, what full and boundless love.

Amen! Amen!
From beginning to end
Christ the story, His the glory
Alleluia! Amen!

Christ, the true and better Moses
Called to lead a people home
Standing bold to earthly powers

God's great glory to be known
With his arms stretched wide to heaven
See the waters part in two
See the veil is torn forever
Cleansed with blood we pass now through.

Christ, the true and better David
Lowly shepherd, mighty King
He the champion in the battle
Where, O death, is now thy sting?
In our place He bled and conquered
Crown Him Lord of majesty
His shall be the throne forever
We shall e'er His people be.

Finally, singing engages the **imagination**. Of course, not all music engages the imagination equally. And some unhelpful worship music engages the imagination in a way that is counterproductive. (I'd rather not think about God's love like a sloppy wet kiss, thank you very much.) But a well-written worship song can engage the imagination and strengthen worship like few other things can. Consider, for example, these lyrics from the classic hymn *Hark, I Hear the Harps Eternal.*

Hark, I hear the harps eternal ringing on the farther shore
As I near those swollen waters with their deep and solemn roar …

And my soul, tho' stain'd with sorrow, fading as the light of day
Passes swiftly o'er those waters, to the city far away …

> Souls have cross'd before me saintly to that land of perfect rest
> And I hear them singing faintly in the mansions of the blest.

As a pastor, one of the main things I do is try to make the hope of heaven stick to the spiritual ribs of my people. I do that in private counseling and public teaching, both of which are utterly indispensable. But it really helps when my people can use their sanctified imagination to see that day as they sing about it on a Sunday morning.

When I sing *Hark, I Hear the Harps Eternal* I think about the saints who have passed before me. I remember their courage, their faith, and even their failures. I imagine them, bruised and bloody from the battles of this fallen world, getting into the boat of Christ's perfect righteousness, passing swiftly over the river from death to life, singing sweetly along the way. I imagine their voices calling out to me from the safety of the further shore, with the harps of God playing a perfect melody as they do. And then I imagine getting into that boat myself one day soon, and hearing that beautiful chorus as I make my own journey, my earthly sorrows fading as the light of day.

And of course, it is not just the great hymn writers (past or present) who engage our imagination with song. God is the original imagination engager. Consider the Song of Moses, one of the earliest songs in Scripture.

God could have merely told the Israelites in rote fashion that He rescued them by causing a wind to separate the waters of the Red Sea. He could have used charts and diagrams to explain the phenomenon. He could have used the Socratic method to dialogue with His people about His wonder working power. But He didn't. Instead, He wrote them a song with lyrics like these:

> At the blast of your nostrils the waters piled up;
> > the floods stood up in a heap;
> > the deeps congealed in the heart of the sea.
>
> (Exod. 15:8)

Can you see it? Can you hear it? Can you … smell it? The nostrils of God blasting winds into the ocean deeps? The waters congealing in the heart of the sea? God doesn't merely want to engage our intellect in worship, He also wants to engage and activate our imagination.

So, yes … God's people sing. We sing because God sings. We sing because God commands us to sing. We sing because we *need* to sing and because we *get* to sing.

So it is my sincere prayer that every member of God's church would grow to truly love to sing praises to the God who made us, the God who loves us, and the God who has saved us.

Much, much more could be said, but we need to move on to the other ten insights.

INSIGHT 2

Sing in Response

Here's a good pocket-sized definition of worship:

> Worship is the right response to the grace of God.

It doesn't matter what form of worship we're talking about:

- Prayer
- Singing
- Giving
- Serving

All of worship is responsive in nature. Consider just a few examples from Scripture:

When God reveals Himself, the people of God respond in worship, just like Moses:

> The LORD passed before him and proclaimed, "The LORD, the LORD, a God merciful and gracious, slow to anger, and abounding in steadfast

> love and faithfulness, keeping steadfast love for thousands, forgiving iniquity and transgression and sin, but who will by no means clear the guilty, visiting the iniquity of the fathers on the children and the children's children, to the third and the fourth generation." And Moses quickly bowed his head toward the earth and worshiped. (Exod. 34:6-8)

And you shouldn't write off Moses' response as exceptional. Consider the book of Nehemiah. When God reveals Himself through the reading and preaching of His Word, the people of God respond in worship, just like when Ezra read the Law to the whole congregation:

> And Ezra opened the book in the sight of all the people, for he was above all the people, and as he opened it all the people stood. And Ezra blessed the LORD, the great God, and all the people answered, "Amen, Amen," lifting up their hands. And they bowed their heads and worshiped the LORD with their faces to the ground ... And the Israelites separated themselves from all foreigners and stood and confessed their sins and the iniquities of their fathers. And they stood up in their place and read from the Book of the Law of the LORD their God for a quarter of the day; for another quarter of it they made confession and worshiped the Lord their God. (Neh. 8:5-6, 9:2-3)

When God answers prayers, His people respond in worship, just like Hannah and Eli:

> And when [Hannah] had weaned [Samuel], she took him up with her, along with a three-year-old bull, an ephah of flour, and a skin of wine, and she brought him to the house of the LORD at Shiloh. And the child was young. Then they slaughtered the bull, and they brought the child to Eli. And she said, "Oh, my lord! As you live, my lord, I am the woman who was standing here in your presence, praying to the LORD. For this child I prayed, and the LORD has granted me my petition that I made to him. Therefore I have lent him to the LORD. As long as he lives, he is lent to the LORD." And [Eli] worshiped the LORD there. (1 Sam. 1:24-28)

And when God *doesn't* answer prayers the way His people had hoped, they still respond in worship, just like David after the death of his infant son:

> But when David saw that his servants were whispering together, David understood that the child was dead. And David said to his servants, "Is the child dead?" They said, "He is dead." Then David arose from the earth and washed and anointed himself and changed his clothes. And he went into the house of the LORD and worshiped. (2 Sam. 12:19-20)

And, of course, when the Son of God reveals His glory through His words and actions, the people of God can't help but respond in worship:

> When [the wise men] saw the star, they rejoiced exceedingly with great joy. And going into

> the house, they saw the child with Mary his mother, and they fell down and worshiped him. Then, opening their treasures, they offered him gifts, gold and frankincense and myrrh. (Matt. 2:10-11)
>
> But when [Peter] saw the wind, he was afraid, and beginning to sink he cried out, "Lord, save me." Jesus immediately reached out his hand and took hold of him, saying to him, "O you of little faith, why did you doubt?" And when they got into the boat, the wind ceased. And those in the boat worshiped him, saying, "Truly you are the Son of God." (Matt. 14:30-33)
>
> "He is not here, for he has risen, as he said. Come, see the place where he lay. Then go quickly and tell his disciples that he has risen from the dead…" So they departed quickly from the tomb with fear and great joy, and ran to tell his disciples. And behold, Jesus met them and said, "Greetings!" And they came up and took hold of his feet and worshiped him. (Matt. 28:6-9)

We see the same pattern in our text. Exodus 15:1 begins with the word "then." This word connects chapter 15 to the events recounted in chapter 14.

What happened in chapter 14? Well, God's people were saved.

Then, in chapter 15, they begin to sing. Do you see? The song is responsive in nature.

Have you ever wondered why so many churches have a hymn of response after the sermon? This is why! After we spend time meditating on our great salvation together, we respond to God by praising Him for His salvation!

Friends, you should know that this is how all of Christian worship works. Every aspect of our worship is *always* a response to what God has already done.

INSIGHT 3

Sing Together

Look at verse one again.

> Then Moses and the people of Israel sang this song to the Lord.

The wording of this verse tells us that Moses and the people of Israel sang *together*. Why? Because they were saved together. Let me say that again for emphasis: *The people of God sing together because they have been saved together.*

It makes sense, then, that the Psalms regularly command the people of God to sing together, too.

> Oh, magnify the LORD with me,
>   and let us exalt his name together! (Ps. 34:3)

> Let them thank the LORD for his steadfast love,
>   for his wondrous works to the children of man!
> Let them extol him in the congregation of the people,
>   and praise him in the assembly of the elders.
> (Ps. 107:31-32)

> Kings of the earth and all peoples,
> > princes and all rulers of the earth!
> Young men and maidens together,
> > old men and children!
> Let them praise the name of the LORD,
> > for his name alone is exalted;
> > his majesty is above earth and heaven.
> (Ps. 148:11-13)

I could keep going. But instead of citing all of Psalmody, I'll just make a grammatical point. The plural pronouns "us," "we," and "our" are used a whopping 346 times in the Psalms. Why? Because these songs are sung *together*! The Psalms are indeed deeply personal, but we've made a mistake if we miss their corporate nature.

When we turn to our New Testaments, we see the same idea. The two most explicit passages to Christians about singing are Colossians 3:16 and Ephesians 5:18-21. Both passages feature singing *together*.

> Let the word of Christ dwell in you richly, teaching and admonishing one another in all wisdom, singing psalms and hymns and spiritual songs, with thankfulness in your hearts to God. (Col. 3:16)

> [Address] one another in psalms and hymns and spiritual songs, singing and making melody to the Lord with your heart. (Eph. 5:19)

In both these verses Christians are singing to God, but they aren't *only* singing to God. As they sing to God, they are "teaching and admonishing one another" and "addressing one another," too. I could say a lot about what this means, but the point I'm making here is simple: Paul assumes worshiping God through song includes the melding of multiple Christian voices.

Modern western Christians have been trained to think of salvation through the lens of individualism, but the gospel says that God is not *merely* saving individuals for Himself, He's saving a people. Which is why so many of the illustrations for salvation in Scripture are corporate in nature. Consider, for example, the doctrine of adoption.

> ... he predestined us for adoption to himself as sons through Jesus Christ, according to the purpose of his will. (Eph. 1:5)

The gospel says that we were orphans; cold, lost, and alone in the world. But then God the Father, through His Son, adopts us into His family, where we will live with Him forever in a big house with enough rooms for all of our siblings! So whether we're talking about a family or a nation or a church or a flock, the biblical image of salvation is thoroughly corporate in nature.

Sometimes we think about salvation as if we're connected to God in a hermetically sealed tube, when in fact, we are part of a procession of those who have been called by God's grace. So when you think about singing songs of worship to God, learn to think less about *me* and more about *we*.

Of course, you are certainly free to sing songs of praise with your family during devotionals, or alone in the car, or in your time with God in the prayer closet. But the highest priority for Christian singing should be with the people of God as we journey towards the Promised Land *together*.

INSIGHT 4

Sing to God, about God

This point may seem somewhat unnecessary, but sometimes we need to state the obvious: when we sing songs of praise, we should sing them to God. Look at verse one with me once more.

> I will sing *to* the Lord.

The people of Israel are not singing to Moses; they are singing to God. Why? Because He is the one who saved them and, therefore, He is the one who deserves the praise. We sing to the Lord because He is the one who is triumphant, He is the one who saves, He is the one who leads and guides His people. He overthrows our enemies. God is the sole object of our worship because He alone is the founder and perfecter of our faith (Heb. 12:2).

This point needs to be made even more emphatically in this therapeutic, proud, egocentric cultural moment where far too many of our worship songs are more about us than God. Consider the lyrics of *The Father's House*, written by Cory Asbury:

> Sometimes on this journey, I get lost in my mistakes
> What looks to me like weakness is a canvas for your strength
> And my story isn't over, my story's just begun
> And failure won't define me 'cause that's what my Father does
> Yeah, failure won't define me 'cause that's what my Father does.

This song reads much more like a personal journal entry than a song of praise to God. And just in case you think this song is an outlier, let us consider one more song written by Maryanne J. George:

> Sometimes we gotta rise
> Sometimes we gotta fall
> Sometimes we gotta lose ourselves
> To find our way home
> Sometimes we gotta break
> Before we're ever made whole
> Isn't it a journey?
> Isn't it beautiful?

I don't think it's going too far to say that most modern worship songs in the west look like this. They are more "me centered" than "God centered." Many Christians gather in so-called Christian services where they will spend a great deal of time singing praises to themselves instead of to God. Whether they realize that's what they're doing or not.

But if God is the sole object of our worship (and He is), then shouldn't we sing songs that are more about Him than us? Even when we sing about ourselves, we should do so in relation to God, both who He is and what He has done to save us.

So, when you're looking for a new church, or evaluating a new song for Sunday morning, or deciding whether or not to add a song to your Spotify playlist, ask yourself, "Does this song help me to sing *to* God and *about* God, or does it cause me to naval gaze and focus on myself more than the gospel?"

But there's more: Not only should we sing *to* God, but we should also sing *about* God when we sing to Him. How? In what way? Well, thankfully, we see a clear and consistent pattern of vibrant worship in Scripture. What we see, if we're looking carefully, is that God's people sing about God's *character* and His *deeds*, His *name* and His *work*, His *attributes* and His *actions*. You can clearly see this pattern in the Song of Moses. Consider the following.

The character and attributes of God are highlighted in ...

- v.6 where the people sing of the power of God, and in ...

- v.10 where the people sing about the sovereignty of God, and in ...
- v.13 where the people sing about the love of God.

When the Israelites sing the Song of Moses, they sing the attributes of God back to Him. Does this sound like the kind of music you're singing in your local church? Or the kind of music that you enjoy devotionally? If not, why not?

As we look even more closely at the Song of Moses, we see that the people of God not only sing about God's attributes, but His actions, not only His character, but His deeds.

- v.3, they recount how the Lord has gone to war against Pharaoh and all that he represents, on behalf of his people.
- vv.4, 7, the Lord destroys the enemies of Israel and casts them into the sea.
- v.13, the Lord guides His people to their holy abode.

Friends, do you understand that God never gets tired of hearing the greatness of His glory sung back to Him? In the same way that a mother never tires of hearing her children tell her that she's "the best mom ever," to a much greater degree, God never tires of hearing His children singing praises to His holy name.

There's an old contemporary Christian song that says, "I could sing of your love forever." Well, I hope you mean it, because that's exactly what

Sing to God, about God

God wants. He wants to hear us sing about His love forever. And we will. For all of eternity we will make sweet melody as we harmonize the glory of God's love and mercy and grace and wrath and justice and so much more. We will rejoice in the nature and character, the attributes, and actions of God forever and ever as we sing the song of salvation, gathered happily around the throne of the Lamb who was slain.

> And between the throne and the four living creatures and among the elders I saw a Lamb standing, as though it had been slain. [And] the four living creatures and the twenty-four elders fell down before the Lamb, each holding a harp, and golden bowls full of incense, which are the prayers of the saints. And they sang a new song, saying,
>
> > "Worthy are you to take the scroll
> >   and to open its seals,
> > for you were slain, and by your blood you ransomed people for God
> >   from every tribe and language and people and nation,
> > and you have made them a kingdom and priests to our God,
> >   and they shall reign on the earth."
>
> Then I looked, and I heard around the throne and the living creatures and the elders the voice of many angels, numbering myriads of myriads and thousands of thousands, saying with a loud voice,

> "Worthy is the Lamb who was slain,
> to receive power and wealth and wisdom
> and might and honor and glory and
> blessing!"

And I heard every creature in heaven and on earth and under the earth and in the sea, and all that is in them, saying,

> "To him who sits on the throne and to the Lamb
> be blessing and honor and glory and might
> forever and ever!"

And the four living creatures said, "Amen!" and the elders fell down and worshiped. (Rev. 5:6-14)

INSIGHT 5

Sing the Truth

> Your voice may not be of professional standard,
> but it is of confessional standard.
> (Keith Getty)

Again, this may seem obvious, but the songs we sing to God should be true. Why? Well, for starters, because the God whom we love and serve is truth in His very being (Jer. 10:10) and His Word is a perfect reflection of that truth (Ps. 119:142). Moreover, the body of Christ (i.e. the church) is the pillar and buttress of truth (1 Tim. 3:15). It does not, therefore, honor God when His people assemble in His name, but then proceed to sing songs *to* Him and *about* Him that are false. In the same way that it would not be honoring to your spouse to write her a poem about her "lovely brown eyes" if her eyes are actually green, it does not honor God to praise Him for things that are not true of Him.

Take, as an example of what not to sing, lyrics like these from the wildly popular song *Reckless Love*:

> Oh, the overwhelming, never-ending, reckless love of God.

There is nothing in Scripture that communicates the idea that God's love is reckless. To the contrary, Scripture speaks about the love of God as something that was planned with painstaking detail, before the foundation of the world (Eph. 1:4). Therefore, we should not sing these patently false lyrics of praise to God in worship. And the good news is, we don't have to! There are so many biblical and beautiful psalms, hymns, and spiritual songs (Eph. 5:19) that have been written about the love of God that we don't have to sing songs that aren't true.[*] From the book of Psalms in your Bible, to the classic hymns of church history, to the many new and amazing hymns being produced by talented and godly servants of the church, there is no reason to sing something that isn't true to God. We have an embarrassment of riches available to us when it comes to maximally God-glorifying music.

It should also be noted that when we sing things that are false about God, we actually hurt

---

[*] Of course, we should allow for some creative license and poetic flourish in the songs we sing. Even so, we should be very careful to make sure the praises we sing to God are actually true.

one another. Remember, when we sing hymns of praise, we are not only singing to God, but also to one another (Eph 5:19). When we sing false things about God to one another, we are failing to disciple each other well.

In Ephesians 4, Paul says that the church is built up into robust health by speaking the truth in love. This means that speaking falsities does not build up the body in any way, but rather, breaks it down. If we wouldn't be content to speak untrue things to our fellow church members in small groups, one-on-one discipling, or in biblical counseling, let us also resolve not to sing untrue things to one another in worship.

INSIGHT 6

Sing the Whole Counsel of God

Look at vv.15-16.

The Song of Moses speaks to the love of God *and* the justice of God, the wrath of God *and* the grace of God. This, of course, is merely a reflection of the gospel itself. The gospel says that God is both loving *and* merciful. Yes and amen. He loves to forgive. The gospel also says that God will by no means let the guilty go unpunished (Exod. 34:7). And these completely compatible truths should be reflected in the music we sing as a church.
Consider, for example, the lyrics of the hymn *Day of Judgment, Day of Wonders*:

> At His call the dead awaken, Rise to life from earth and sea;
> All the powers of nature shaken, By His look, prepare to flee.
> Careless sinner, what will then become of thee?

Now verse 5.

> But to those who have confessed, Loved and served the Lord below,
> He will say, "Come near, ye blessed, See the kingdom I bestow;
> You for-ever, Shall My love and glory know."

Love *and* justice. Wrath *and* grace.

In Acts 20:27, Paul said that he did not hesitate to *preach* "the whole counsel of God." Likewise, we should not hesitate to *sing* the whole counsel of God.

Think back to the Psalms again. God penned the Psalms through the inspiration of the Holy Spirit so that we might have the right words to pray and sing back to Him. Why, then, did He give us 150 chapters of poems? Surely a handful of praise choruses would have done the job, right? Well, actually no.

Have you ever stopped to consider the breadth of the Psalms? They cover almost every human emotion and almost every significant biblical theme. There are Psalms of praise, Psalms of thanksgiving, Psalms of lament, imprecatory Psalms, royal Psalms, wisdom Psalms, and more.

If you're sad about persecution or the devil or your sin, God has a song of lament for you. If you're glad about God's character and deeds, God has a song of praise for you. If you're going on a nature walk, take Psalm 19 along with you. If you're angry over injustice, remember Psalm 5. Delighting in your children? Psalm 127. Feeling cerebral and contemplative? Psalm 37. Jealous about money? Psalm 73. Thankful for the Word? Psalm 119. Brushing up on your history? Psalm 105.

Hopefully you get the point. God has set His whole counsel to song. So, sing about all of it!

INSIGHT 7

Sing History

... this is my God, and I will praise him,
my father's God, and I will exalt him.
(Exod. 15:2)

In verse 2 of Moses' song, we see that God wants His people to look back at His track record of salvation throughout history. He wants His people to know that He is not merely the savior of Moses, He is also the savior of Joseph, Jacob, Isaac, and Abraham.

Do you know that? Do you understand that God is not merely the savior of this present generation? That He's been saving a people for Himself for thousands of years? Friend, you are just the most recent addition to a long and vibrant lineage of grace. As am I. And we should indeed feel honored to be added to the great multitude. But we must remember that there is in fact a multitude, not just across the globe today, but throughout history.

Redemption Song

The Song of Moses teaches us that we must not forget the saints who came before us. We must not lionize them, to be sure. They were sinners just like us. But we must not forget them either. If we forget the saints of old, we forget a key component of the gospel story.

One of the ways we try to stay connected to the lineage of grace at my local church is by singing songs that span the generations. On any given Sunday morning at 6th Avenue Community Church we may sing a song that is five years old or five hundred years old or five thousand years old.

We sing songs from the twenty-first century, like *In Christ Alone*:

> In Christ alone, my hope is found
> He is my light, my strength, my song
> This Cornerstone, this solid ground
> Firm through the fiercest drought and storm
> What heights of love, what depths of peace
> When fears are stilled, when strivings cease
> My Comforter, my all in all
> Here in the love of Christ I stand.

We sing songs from the nineteenth century, like *It Is Well*:

> When peace, like a river, attendeth my way,
> When sorrows like sea billows roll;
> Whatever my lot, Thou hast taught me to say,
> It is well, it is well with my soul.

Sing History

> It is well (It is well),
> With my soul (With my soul)
> It is well, it is well, with my soul.

We sing songs from the eighteenth century, like *Come, Thou Fount of Every Blessing*:

> Come, Thou Fount of every blessing
> Tune my heart to sing Thy grace
> Streams of mercy, never ceasing
> Call for songs of loudest praise
> Teach me some melodious sonnet
> Sung by flaming tongues above
> Praise the mount, I'm fixed upon it
> Mount of Thy redeeming love.

We sing songs from the sixteenth century, like *A Mighty Fortress*:

> A mighty fortress is our God, a bulwark never failing
> Our Helper He, amid the flood of mortal ills prevailing
> For still our ancient foe doth seek to work us woe
> His craft and pow'r are great, and, armed with cruel hate
> On earth is not his equal.

And we sing the psalms, written long before Christ:

> Praise the LORD.
> Praise God in his sanctuary;
>   praise him in his mighty heavens.

> Praise him for his acts of power;
> praise him for his surpassing greatness
> Praise him with the sounding of the trumpet,
> praise him with the harp and lyre,
> praise him with timbrel and dancing,
> praise him with the strings and pipe,
> praise him with the clash of cymbals,
> praise him with resounding cymbals.
> Let everything that has breath praise the LORD.
> Praise the LORD.
> (Ps. 150 NIV)
>
> Why, my soul, are you downcast?
> Why so disturbed within me?
> Put your hope in God,
> for I will yet praise him,
> my Savior and my God.
> (Ps. 42:5 NIV)

Singing about the saints of old unites us to them in a song of grace that not only reaches back into history, but that will also echo throughout eternity. It is an honor, a privilege, and a duty to make sure that we sing the gospel in a way that looks back on our forefathers in the faith. Consider, for example, these lyrics from the hymn *Let Us Love and Sing And Wonder*. (Don't move past them too quickly. Sit with them. Meditate on them. Be moved to worship by them!)

> Let us praise and join the chorus
> of the saints enthroned on high,
> here they trusted him before us,
> now their praises fill the sky.

INSIGHT 8

Sing as a Leader

King David was a man after God's own heart. And he made a habit of leading the people in praise. In fact, there is no place he would rather be than in the temple worshiping God, "For a day in your courts is better than a thousand elsewhere. I would rather be a doorkeeper in the house of my God than dwell in the tents of wickedness" (Ps. 84:10). In one scene, David literally leads a procession of worshipers in his underwear! He was doing everything in his power to will the people to sing and dance and worship with everything they have.

> And David danced before the LORD with all his might. And David was wearing a linen ephod. So David and all the house of Israel brought up the ark of the LORD with shouting and with the sound of the horn. (2 Sam. 6:14-15)

King Hezekiah, one of the few good kings to follow in David's footsteps, also led the way in worship.

He brought the people of Israel back to the Word of God, and along with the Word came worship. But he didn't just command the people to praise God while he went about his own business. No way! He led the way in worship, bowing down to the Lord before all the people.

> Then Hezekiah commanded that the burnt offering be offered on the altar. And when the burnt offering began, the song to the Lord began also, and the trumpets, accompanied by the instruments of David king of Israel. The whole assembly worshiped, and the singers sang, and the trumpeters sounded. All this continued until the burnt offering was finished. When the offering was finished, the king and all who were present with him bowed themselves and worshiped. And Hezekiah the king and the officials commanded the Levites to sing praises to the LORD with the words of David and of Asaph the seer. And they sang praises with gladness, and they bowed down and worshiped. (2 Chron. 29:27-30)

King David and King Hezekiah aren't alone in leading the way in worship. They take after Moses who came before them. Notice the way verse 1 reads. It says, "Moses *and* the people." This is like saying, "The pastor and the church." When it comes to corporate worship, Moses is leading by example from the front.

Which does not necessarily mean that Moses had the best voice in the congregation. Or that

Sing as a Leader

he knew music theory better than everyone else. He might have. But probably not. Which is fine, because the heart of leadership has less to do with talent and technical prowess and more to do with setting an example of worshiping in spirit and truth, with love and enthusiasm.

Think about how this applies to various leaders in a congregation. Take elders, for example. If a man aspires to be a pastor in God's church, he must be a role model of godly worship. Not from the stage, but from right there in your pew. Speaking as a pastor, I can't imagine appointing someone to a position of pastoral leadership in the church who prays half-heartedly, or who listens to a sermon disinterestedly, or who sings with a lackluster spirit. A pastor should be someone that anyone in the church can look to as an example of what it looks like to follow Jesus. And if I can't point to a man and say, "That's how you praise God in song!" then he's probably not pastor material.[*]

Ok, now let's think about how this applies to other leaders in the church. Dads, think about how this applies to you. You set the tone for your family's singing. Your children may end up singing well even if you don't, but that will be God's work in them despite your leadership, not because of it. Ask

---

[*] By this I do not mean that he must be the most joyful, or tearful, or animated and exuberant during singing. I mean something more like, "This man is meaningfully engaged."

yourself this question that I like to ask new fathers in our church. If your children grow up to worship God the way you do on a Sunday morning, would you be proud of their worship? Would they sing heartily and happily? Or would they be passive, dreary, and disinterested participants?

Listen to me, men. You were created to lead, and you were created to sing. Your Father God sings (Zeph. 3:17), and so should you. I understand that much of the modern evangelical church has been feminized in its music ministry which can make singing feel awkward and unnatural for men. That needs to change. But you must be an active part of the solution, not a grumbling addition to the problem. You must insist on reclaiming the human voice as an instrument in the war against sin and hell and death. Act like a man (1 Cor. 16:13) and sing like a warrior going out to battle, because in a very real sense, that's who you are (2 Tim. 2:1-4).

Lest my sisters feel left out, let's think about how this applies to women, who are called to be leaders in the church as well.

> Older women likewise are to be reverent in behavior, not slanderers or slaves to much wine. They are to teach what is good, and so train the young women to love their husbands and children, to be self-controlled, pure, working at home, kind, and submissive to their own husbands, that the word of God may not be reviled. (Titus 2:3-5)

Sing as a Leader

Every woman in the church should aspire to be a Titus 2 woman, the kind of woman who trains younger women in what it looks like to follow Jesus *as a woman*. And singing is a part of that. To my sisters in Christ, do you understand that younger women in the church are looking at you to see what it looks like to worship God? When they look at you, what do they see?

At the very end of the Song of Moses, we see Miriam held up as an example of godly feminine worship.

> Then Miriam the prophetess, the sister of Aaron, took a tambourine in her hand, and all the women went out after her with tambourines and dancing. And Miriam sang to them:
>
> > "Sing to the LORD, for he has triumphed gloriously;
> > the horse and his rider he has thrown into the sea." (Exod. 15:20-21)

Miriam was a Titus 2 woman before Titus 2 was written. She was so moved by the great salvation of God that she had to respond in worship. And when she did, she was an example to the younger women watching her. More than that, Miriam used music to encourage and strengthen her sisters. She sang to them as she called on them to join her in offering praise to God. She invited her sisters to join in the song of salvation with her.

You don't have to play an instrument to be a Miriam, and you certainly don't have to dance, but you should have the same heart as Miriam, desiring that the younger women in the church "go out after you" as you role model what it looks like to sing praises to God from a place of deep and serious joy.

INSIGHT 9

Sing to Bear Witness

A testimony is a public declaration of salvation. Christians should love to share their testimony, and they should also love to hear and be encouraged by the testimonies of others. Every testimony offers a fresh experience of the gospel as it is rehearsed in the context of different stories. Testimonies are often shared before baptisms, during church services, and at special ministry events. But the Song of Moses also shows us that the people of God can sing their testimony, because—after all—the Song of Moses is a testimony set to music.

If this idea is new to you, go back and reread the text. Look at the language of the song. Doesn't this song sound just like a testimony that you might hear in your local church? All testimonies are just different versions of the same story: I was facing certain destruction, but then God came in and saved me by His grace. And now I want to praise

His name in public, even as I wait for Him to lead me all the way home. That's your story. That's my story. That's the story of every blood-bought sinner, from the dawning days of Israel to the setting sun of human history (Rev. 12:11).

When you give your testimony, do you talk like this? Does your story sound like this song? Do you give *God* all the glory for the things He alone has done? Do you highlight *His* nature and character? Do you speak of *His* mighty deeds? Or do you talk about yourself? Who is the hero of your story?

Some of the most powerful songs in church history allow us to make much of God, with one voice, as we sing of our great salvation together. One of my all-time favorite hymns is called *Victory in Jesus*. We sing it at every baptism in my church, and for good reason. I share it with you below in hopes that your church loves it as much as mine, and sings it (with other songs like it) more and more often as the day draws near.

> I heard an old old story
> How a Savior came from glory
> How He gave His life on Calvary
> To save a wretch like me
> I heard about His groaning
> Of His precious blood's atoning
> Then I repented of my sins
> And won the victory.

Sing to Bear Witness

Oh, victory in Jesus
My Savior, forever
He sought me and bought me
With His redeeming blood
He loved me ere I knew Him
And all my love is due Him
He plunged me to victory
Beneath the cleansing flood.

I heard about His healing
Of His cleansing pow'r revealing
How He made the lame to walk again
And caused the blind to see
And then I cried, 'Dear Jesus
Come and heal my broken spirit'
And somehow Jesus came and brought
To me the victory.

I heard about a mansion
He has built for me in glory
And I heard about the streets of gold
Beyond the crystal sea
About the angels singing
And the old redemption story
And some sweet day I'll sing up there
The song of victory.

INSIGHT 10

Sing in Wonder

John Newton's classic hymn *Amazing Grace* has become so familiar to us that we may forget that the point of the song is to help us, with fresh eyes, to be amazed by God. Which is good, because God's grace often fails to amaze us when we become accustomed to it.

The Israelites were amazed by the grace of God as they sang the Song of Moses together. They were absolutely stunned. They could see, with fresh clear eyes, the wonder of God's loving kindness. Look at verse eleven with this reality in mind.

> Who is like you, O Lord, among the gods?
> Who is like you, majestic in holiness,
> awesome in glorious deeds, doing wonders?
> (Exod. 15:11)

When was the last time you talked about God like this? When was the last time you thought about

God like this? When was the last time that the God of your salvation stunned you and left you wondering at His glory?

When you sing on a Sunday morning, are you actually thinking about what you're singing, meditating and wondering at the nature and character of God, or are you just passively mouthing the words? I know I have certainly caught myself, on more than one occasion, moving my lips without engaging my heart. If we're being honest, we've probably all been there.

It's kind of like when you're reading a book and you realize that your eyes have been moving along the page but your mind hasn't been engaging with the content. In the same way, our eyes can scan the lyrics, and our mouths can move with the words, without our heart ever engaging with God in sincere praise. When you realize that this is happening, what do you do? Hopefully, you re-engage!

When you catch yourself singing without *really* singing, here's what you do. First of all, don't beat yourself up. We've all been there. You're only human. But also, don't give yourself a pass on dispassionate praise (which is really no praise at all). Instead, pinch yourself (metaphorically, that is), and recenter your heart. Refocus. Meditate on the gospel, and get back to singing to God with your whole heart.

In 1 Corinthians, Paul tells the church that he will "sing praise with his spirit." Great. But he doesn't stop there. He goes on to say, "But I will sing with my mind also." (1 Cor. 14:15). This is instructive for us today. We must engage every part of our being when we worship God. If we love God with all of our heart, soul, mind, and strength (Mark 12:30), then that means that we should sing to Him with all of our heart, soul, mind, and strength. Give us grace to do it, Lord!

Before moving on to the next principle, take a moment to wonder at God with me. Read these lyrics from *Amazing Grace*, and let them move you to deep joy and great wonder in the gospel.

> When we've been there ten thousand years,
>   Bright shining as the sun,
> We've no less days to sing God's praise
>   Than when we first begun.

Are you not absolutely blown away by this picture of heaven? When we've been there, in heaven, with God, basking in His glory, praising His holy name, for ten thousand years, it will feel like we're just getting started. Wow.

When you meditate on the gospel, let it move you to wonder at God. Paul does. After eleven chapters of Gospel meditation in the book of Romans, Paul has to pause to reflect and wonder at the wisdom of God:

> Oh, the depth of the riches and wisdom and knowledge of God! How unsearchable are his judgments and how inscrutable his ways! (Rom. 11:33)

INSIGHT 11

Sing with Joy

This final point may be more challenging than all of the rest combined, and I'll tell you why: We are called to sing with joy. God is not honored by joyless singing, in the same way that a lover is not honored by perfunctory affection. The lover wants to be rejoiced in. But what can you do when you don't feel joy? At the end of the day, joy is not something that we can produce in ourselves by sheer will of force.

As a pastor, I wish I could just push a button in the hearts of all my church members that makes them automatically rejoice in God as they sing. I wish I could do that for my own heart! But that's not the way emotions work. And that's not the kind of worship God wants anyways. He doesn't want our worship to be programmed or performative, He wants our worship to be freely given as an overflow of our deep love for Him.

So, how do we find joy in our singing?

In his fantastic song *Penelope Judd*, Shai Linne tells us the story of a little girl who lived with the mud children. Shai tells us that Penelope was a "sad sad girl" because she lived in a "bad bad world …

> Where kids teased each other and acted really mean
> They lied, cheated and stole, and their speech was obscene
> With no grown-ups around, nobody was really wise
> So every kid did what was right in their own eyes
> Penelope would cry—like every single day
> No matter what she did, the tears wouldn't go away.

Well, one day, Penelope heard the news that there was a king who lived on a great mountain top. And the king, being a proud father, was throwing a huge party in his son's honor.

And then something incredible happened. A dove came to Penelope to tell her that she was officially invited to the king's banquet.

As Penelope set out on her journey to the castle of the great king, she waved goodbye to all the mud children who mocked her and laughed at her decision to leave.

The dove would guide Penelope on her journey, singing to her all along the way:

Sing with Joy

> Off we go with no delay
> Don't let nobody try to make you stay
> We're gonna see the King, we're on our way
> And all the old things gonna pass away.

Beginning the journey was difficult for Penelope. Part of her wanted to stay. But then, finally, she came to herself and said…

> "Why would I want to stay?
> Because all they do is play in the mud all day
> And while they're doing that, I'm gonna see the King!"
> It made Penelope so happy, she started to sing.

It made her so happy she started to sing.

This, brothers and sisters, is how we sing with joy. When we meditate on our lost state as children of the mud, and how God, through His gospel, has made a way for us to be with Him again, we can't help but sing with joy!

You don't get Christians to sing with joy by telling them how they ought to feel about God, you get them to sing for joy by telling them *about God*! And if they really love Him, if they really love His glory, if His grace is really amazing to them, they will respond with great joy.

Think about what the Israelites have experienced at this point in the exodus story. They have passed safely through the waters of the Red Sea that represent sin, death, and hell. And when they get to the other side, they respond by making a joyful noise to the Lord. Of course they do! They were facing certain death and destruction, and then God miraculously saved them.

Friend, if you don't see yourself the same way, as someone who has been miraculously saved, you will never be able to sing with the kind of joy that only belief in the gospel can give. *You* were facing certain death and destruction. *You* were dead in your trespasses and sins. *You* were on your way to hell. *You* were facing the wrath of God forever. But then Jesus, the greater Moses, parted the waters of death on your behalf. He was drowned by the wrath of the Father on the cross so that you wouldn't be swallowed up in the waters of God's perfect justice. Jesus was treated like Pharaoh and his armies so that you could be saved like Moses and the people of Israel. So sing, brothers and sisters, as the old hymn reminds us.

> So sing with joy, afflicted one;
> The battle's fierce, but the victory's won!

Doxology

The Song of Moses is an amazing song, and its beautiful truths will echo down the halls of the mansion of the blessed for all of eternity. Consider these words from Revelation 15:

> And they sing the song of Moses, the servant of God, and the song of the Lamb, saying,
>
> > "Great and amazing are your deeds,
> >   O Lord God the Almighty!
> > Just and true are your ways,
> >   O King of the nations!
> > Who will not fear, O Lord,
> >   and glorify your name?
> > For you alone are holy.
> >   All nations will come
> >   and worship you,
> > for your righteous acts have been revealed."
> > (Rev. 15:3-4)

Don't wait until heaven, my friends, to worship Jesus in spirit and truth. Give Him the honor and glory *today*, in your prayer closet, in your family devotionals, and in your local church, by worshiping Him according to His Word. He has not left us without guidance. He has called us to worship His holy name, and He has shown us how to do so faithfully. He even writes sample songs for us! So sing like the gospel is real and you have been saved by it. Sing like Jesus is Lord and His Word is sufficient. Sing like the Spirit lives in you and is guiding you home. Sing like you are both an exile in a foreign land and a citizen of the celestial city, because that's exactly who you are. Sing the Song of Moses, the song of the Lamb, to a lost and dying world that desperately needs to hear the soundtrack of redemption.

APPENDIX 1

The Regulative Principle

The Necessity of the Regulative Principle
Here's a pocket-sized definition of the regulative principle.

> The Word of God regulates the worship of God for the people of God.

This definition doesn't capture every nuance and facet of the regulative principle, but it gets to the heart of the matter in a way that most non-scholars can grasp and remember.

The easiest way to get off on the wrong foot in an appendix on the regulative principle is to get technical—to break out definitions, charts, and all things academic. I'm not going to do that to you. For now, the main thing that I want us to understand about the regulative principle is this: Not only has God called us to worship Him, but He has *also* given us everything we need to worship Him well (if only we will have eyes to see and ears to hear).

What comes to mind when you think of the term Regulative Principle? For many Christians, the regulative principle is nothing more than a list of rules, synonymous for all the things we *can't* do in worship. To be clear, it's not entirely wrong to think about biblical worship having rules. Christians must understand that the rules and boundaries God has given us in worship actually help facilitate strong, healthy, vibrant worship—not get in the way of it.

Consider this by way of analogy: Think about a game that you love to play, whichever game you prefer. In order for that game to be played *well*, you need a referee, a rule set, and penalties for rule violations. A game with no rules is pure chaos and not edifying for anyone involved. To an infinitely greater degree, the same thing is true of biblical worship. The rules, boundaries, and penalties help facilitate good, true, and beautiful worship that is edifying for everyone involved (the saints) and glorifying to our main audience (God).

Nevertheless, when we talk about the regulative principle, framing is everything. You can talk about the right thing in the wrong way, and we want to avoid that when talking about something as important as biblical worship. What we need to do is show our people—and we need to see ourselves—that when God regulates our worship, He does so to give us *more* of the good, the true, and the beautiful, not *less*. He regulates our worship according to His Word because He cares for us, because He wants us to have the maximum joy possible *in Him* through our worship. And who knows better than God what kind of worship will best serve His people? No one.

We also need to show our people that, left to our own devices, we will *always* drift towards sin and compromise in worship. Think about the golden calf incident at the foot of Mount Sinai (Exod. 32:4). Left to their own devices, the people of Israel began to worship God according to *their own view* of the good, true, and beautiful, and it cost them dearly (Exod. 32:27-28).

Or think about the church in Corinth. Left to their own devices, their worship became more me-centered than God-centered. They only cared about the most prominent gifts (1 Cor. 12–13). They corrupted the Lord's Supper with debauchery (1 Cor 11:17-24). They failed to honor headship and submission in their gatherings (1 Cor 11:2-16), etc. And in so doing, they robbed themselves of the fullness of joy and beauty that should have been theirs in Christ.

So, if we sinners are going to worship a holy and righteous God, we need the regulative principle. But how does it work? What does the regulative principle look like in the life of the local church? I'm glad you asked.

How It Works

Here's how this works: God, in His Word, gives us foundational principles, and then expects us to apply said principles in wisdom and prudence. (The more technical terms that theologians have used here are *forms* and *elements*. Which is fine! I prefer to speak of *principles* and *prudence* because I'm a Baptist pastor who can't stop alliterating to save his life.)

Sometimes biblical principles for worship are stated explicitly. For example:

> I do not permit a woman to teach or exercise authority over a man. (1 Tim 2:12)

That one's pretty straightforward. It's the principle of male headship in the church. Sometimes, however, principles are not stated explicitly, but rather, must be derived implicitly by good and necessary consequence. For example, Ephesians 5 tells us not to get drunk with wine, but rather, be filled with the Spirit (Eph. 5:18). The explicit command here is not to get drunk with alcohol, but an implied, deeper principle is also that we are to not intoxicate ourselves with any other substance (e.g. heroine, ecstasy, cocaine, etc.).

An example of this kind of implied principle for worship is the command to sing psalms, hymns and spiritual songs *to one another*. The *explicit* command given is that Christians sing *to one another*, but *implied* in this command is all of the prudential questions that help or hinder us from singing to one another well. How can we sing to *one another* if, for example, we can't see or hear one another? Lighting and volume are not addressed *explicitly* in this text, but can be *implied* by good and necessary consequence.

Finally, we should note that some biblical principles for worship are neither stated *explicitly* nor *implied*, but rather, are *derived* from a right understanding of patterns found in Scripture. For example: It is a pattern in Scripture that God's people sing *together*. Consider…

> Then Moses and *the people of Israel* sang this song to the Lord, saying … (Exod. 15:1)

Or …

> I will give thanks to the Lord with my whole heart,
>   in the company of the upright, *in the congregation*.
> (Ps. 111:1)

While we are certainly free to sing songs of praise to God individually, one of the core principles of biblical worship (as evidenced by patterns of practice throughout the storyline of salvation) is that we not only sing, but that we sing *together*.

The Flexibility of the Regulative Principle
The regulative principle is firm, but *flexible*.

As an avid CrossFitter, I've found over the years that CrossFit has been, to my mind, unfairly criticized in a number of ways. People say things like, "It's expensive," or "It's a cult!" or "You'll get hurt working out like that." But none of these critiques are necessarily inherent to the CrossFit system. CrossFit, as a fitness program, is nothing more or less than "constantly varied, functional movements, performed at a high intensity." And you can do "constantly varied, functional movements, performed at a high intensity" a thousand different ways which are not expensive, dangerous, or cult-like.

For example, I know several elderly people who use CrossFit for longevity purposes. They don't do super heavy deadlifts or walk on their hands like professional CrossFit athletes do, and yet, they do the same *kind* of training. The principles are the same, even if prudence dictates that the practice varies according to the physical limitations of the elderly. For example, rather than performing heavy barbell squats, elderly CrossFitters will perform box squats using just their body weight. Or, instead of box jumps (which can be hard on the knees and dangerous for the shins) they will perform box step-ups. You get the point ...

The regulative principle in worship is kind of like CrossFit: You should be able to adapt its core principles to any context using wisdom and prudence. To say it another way, *if the regulative principle is biblical*, you should be able to plug it into any church context, anywhere in the world, at any point in history, and see it work.

- A late Victorian puritan church,
- A predominately black church on the southside of Chicago,
- A Korean presbyterian church in the 1800s, or even…
- A church like the one I was a member of in the middle of the amazon jungles of Peru.

If the regulative principle is true and biblical (and I think it is) then I can't imagine a church context wherein I would say, "The culture and context of this church is so unique that its worship doesn't need to be regulated by the Word of God."

- Rich church, poor church.
- Black church, Asian church.
- Rural church, big city church.
- A church on the frontier of the mission field or a long-established church.
- Baptist, Presbyterian, or Anglican.

Every church needs to have its worship regulated by the Word of God. But the way that the Word governs will take a unique shape depending on its context. And that's by design! God built the system to be flexible because He knew that His gospel would go out to all peoples, tongues, tribes, and nations (Rev. 7:9) and that a one-size-fits-all approach to worship would never work in such a beautifully diverse world.

Christians will always, to some extent, disagree about which practice is *most* wise in any particular context. This is not only to be expected, but is also part of the fun of the regulative principle. We get to figure it out *together*! And not tear each other to shreds over it … right?

Right.

The Beauty of the Regulative Principle

So far we've seen the necessity and the flexibility of the regulative principle, but now we must consider perhaps the most important element of all: the beauty.

The final point to be made in this brief appendix on the regulative principle is this: beauty is not in the eye of the beholder; beauty is what God says it is.

Very often, when people come into contact with the regulative principle, they are *initially* repulsed by it. They think it's dry, or boring, and certainly not beautiful. And maybe *sometimes* they're right. Not everyone who tries to rightly order the church's worship does a good job of it. But more often than not, the problem isn't the worship, it's the tastes of the worshiper. That is, their tastes are more carnal than biblical. They are childish in their thinking, not mature. Their sensibilities need to be calibrated by the Word of God, having been more corrupted than they realize by the world and it's *fallen* standards of the good, true, and *beautiful*.

Growing up I used to think that Taco Bell was really good Mexican food. Objectively, I was wrong. I needed to have my palate calibrated. In the same way, people who come from certain church contexts may say things like, "I like the preaching at this church, but the music isn't very good." Maybe. Or, maybe our standards of beauty in worship need to be adjusted.

We would do well to remember that God's designs for worship are always more beautiful than ours. When churches worship God in ways that are in opposition to His Word—no matter the aesthetic, no matter the quality of the musicianship, no matter the skill of the lighting technicians, or the emotional experience of those in attendance—if worship is not *biblical*, it is not *beautiful*.

We strive, therefore, to align our vision of beauty to God's vision of beauty by seeking out God's definition of beauty in His Word.

APPENDIX 2

Case Studies on the Flexibility of the Regulative Principle

I'd like for us to spend some time considering examples of the flexibility of the regulative principle in worship. We're going to do this by considering various elements of a Sunday morning worship service (principles) and how they can be applied in wisdom (prudence).

Principle #1: Preaching

Paul tells Timothy to ...

Preach the Word. (2 Tim. 4:2)

We also see, as a pattern in the New Testament, that the preaching of God's Word is the heartbeat of the church. Paul tells the church in Rome, for example, that he wants to visit them so that he might strengthen them by his preaching (Rom. 1:15). We are not only saved by the preaching of the gospel (Rom. 10:14) but we are also sustained by it.

So, the Bible clearly and consistently, explicitly and implicitly, and by way of pattern, prescribes the preaching of God's Word to God's people. But here's a list of things related to preaching that the Bible leaves to wisdom and prudence. For example, how long should a sermon be? Should I preach from a manuscript or extemporaneously? How many illustrations should be used? Which format is best? How much application should be given?

These questions are not prescribed answers. Rather, they are left up to the wisdom and prudence of the pastor. Every preacher must ask himself, "What is the best way for me to communicate the point of the passage to my people in gospel power?"

Ok, now let's do…

Principle #2: Scripture Reading
Paul tells Timothy in 1 Timothy 4 …

> devote yourself to the public reading of Scripture. (1 Tim. 4:13)

Ok, so we know from this text (and a few others!) that Scripture reading is a prescribed element of our corporate worship. But how much Scripture should be read on a Sunday morning? A whole book? Just one verse? How long should the reading be? What percentage of our service should be given to the reading of the Word: 5 percent or 50 percent or 100 percent? If it's 100 percent, we won't have room for other Word ministries, like singing the Word, preaching the Word, and so forth. But if it's just 1 percent of our service, well, what are we really gathering around? Whose words are we actually listening to?

Ok, let's say that we want 20 percent of our service to be Scripture reading. How should we disperse the Scripture reading throughout the service? Should we front-load it? Or back-load it? Or ... middle ... load it?

Or, consider the question of Bible translation: Which version of the Bible should we read from when we read Scripture in our services? Should the Scripture reader stand behind a pulpit or read from his or her seat? Should the reading be dramatized, to bring it to life? Or should it be read less dynamically, to make sure we're not manipulating people's emotions? I know of a church that reads one chapter of the Bible every Sunday in an attempt to read through the whole bible continuously over the course of several years. Should we do that?

In my home church, we read Scripture that reinforces the main point of the text, as well as scriptural calls to worship, calls to repentance, assurances of pardon, and benedictions. Does the regulative principle say they're right and we're wrong, or vice versa? I don't think so. The regulative principle says, "Make the reading of God's Word an important part of your worship, and wisdom and prudence will dictate how you can do that for maximum edification in your culture and context."

Ok, now let's do prayer…

Principle #3: Prayer

Consider these two verses.

> And they devoted themselves to the apostles' teaching and the fellowship, to the breaking of bread and the **prayers**. (Acts 2:42)

> Again I say to you, if two of you agree on earth about anything they **ask**, it will be done for them by my Father in heaven. For where two or three are gathered in my name, there am I among them. (Matt. 18:19-20)

Ok, so praying should *definitely* be a part of our corporate worship. But as far as I'm aware, there's no one-size-fits-all template for prayers in Sunday service. Not in my New Testament, anyways. But that doesn't mean that we don't have *any* guidance from Scripture. For example, Scripture models several different kinds of prayer for the body of Christ, like praise, petition, confession, and lament.

Scripture doesn't tell me that I have to pray all of these types of prayer every Sunday, but if Scripture is full of these kinds of prayers, then doesn't it seem wise to strive to pray them on a fairly regular basis?

Scripture also very clearly tells us the kinds of things we should be praying for. Consider, for example, The Lord's Prayer. We ought to pray for daily bread and the will of the Lord to be done on earth (Matt. 6:9-13). Or, consider the example of Paul's prayers. He almost never prays for health issues, but always seems to be deep in prayer over gospel issues (Rom. 1:16-23). We would do well to carefully consider how these various prayer patterns should inform our corporate prayers on Sunday morning.

What about the length of our prayers? There's no clear command in Scripture as to how long a prayer should be—a five-minute prayer may be more God-honoring than a five-hour prayer given what Jesus says about vain repetition (Matt. 6:7).

Scripture says that *all things* should be done for the edification of the body (1 Cor. 14:26). When I first arrived at the local church I currently pastor, a five-minute prayer was asking a lot of our people. Several five-minute prayers was pushing them to their limit. But in early puritan settlements, a minister might have been fired for praying less than an hour on a Sunday morning. Context matters.

What about notes? Should our prayers be written in advance or should they be extemporaneous? Well, I can think of a church context where extemporaneous prayers might be truly powerful and edifying! But I can also think of a church context where the last thing I would ever do is open up the microphone on a Sunday morning for *ad hoc* prayer time. Lord, give us wisdom!

Let's keep going. What about…

Principle #4: The Lord's Supper
How often should the Lord's Supper be? I know that there will be some disagreements on this question among Bible believing Christians, but the closest thing I've seen to a prescription in the New Testament is this:

> As often as you do this. (1 Cor. 11:25-26)

What about the finer details of the elements? Should we use gluten-free bread to accommodate gluten intolerance? Should we have our people walk up the aisle to get the elements, or should we disperse the elements to people in the pews? (I've heard really good arguments for the latter pertaining to accountability, but I still think this falls into the principle/wisdom category.) Should the congregation sing a song during communion or observe solemn silence? Scripture doesn't say!

The one thing we do know quite clearly from Scripture is that the Lord's Supper is only for believers to celebrate as an ongoing oath sign of their covenant with Christ and one another (1 Cor. 10:17). We also know from 1 Corinthians that a Spirit of selfishness is so out of sync with the

Lord's supper that Paul says that if a church eats in selfishness rather than love it's not even really celebrating the Lord's Supper at all (1 Cor. 11:20).

Ok, now let's talk about…

Principle #5: Singing

> … addressing one another in psalms and hymns and spiritual songs, singing and making melody to the Lord with your heart. (Eph. 5:19)

> Let the word of Christ dwell in you richly, teaching and admonishing one another in all wisdom, singing psalms and hymns and spiritual songs, with thankfulness in your hearts to God. (Col. 3:16)

Here's the idea: The Word of Christ should dwell so richly in our worship that it spills the banks of our hearts, over our lips, and into song. And not just to the Lord, but also to one another.

So what would the regulative principle have to say about the flexibility of the command to sing to one another? How many songs should we sing on a Sunday morning? I've been in churches that sing ten songs every service. My local church sings four and the doxology. So, five. How long or short should the songs be? Should there be a choir? Should there be a music leader? Should the music leader stand in front of the congregation, or off to the side, or behind them?

And what about drums? The text doesn't say anything about drums. So, are we free to use them? Well, that depends. How loud are the drums? If your instruments are so loud that you can't hear the congregation singing, that's a problem.

Recently, while on sabbatical, I visited several churches with bands so loud that I couldn't hear myself singing, much less my neighbors, thus making it literally impossible to fulfill the command to sing to one another.

But, I also visited a gathering in Chicago with three hundred men singing their guts out in the most acoustically perfect room ever invented. There was a guitar, a keyboard, and yes, drums, and I had zero issues hearing my neighbors singing. (Context matters. Lord, give us wisdom!)

Some churches put their drums in a big, plexiglass box to dampen the sound. Others use electronic drums so that they can lower the volume in the sound booth. I once visited a church where one of the musicians had built a contraption that had a kick-pedal cajon, soft snare, and a single high hat. It added the perfect amount of percussion to the music without overpowering the singing.

What about the number of instruments? Well, I've seen a church use only a guitar or piano and sing the most amazingly beautiful and edifying music. I've also seen churches with seven-piece ensembles that were in no way edifying to anyone who wasn't on stage. The trumpet player was the pastor's niece, the bass player was a legacy deacon, the guitar player was mediocre but still led in music because he threw a fit the last time the worship leader tried to replace him. And so, the church had to deal with several unskilled musicians playing very poorly with one another every Sunday to the edification of very few in the congregation.

What about lighting? It's really hard to sing to one another when we can't see one another. Moreover, when every part of the meeting hall is dark except the stage, we unwittingly communicate the idea that the stage is the place where the singing really matters.

I could keep going, but I think you get the point. The regulative principle is firm, but flexible. And that's by design. There's no one order of service that has been ordained by God to work in every context. But there are certain elements of worship, principles, rules … whatever you want to call them … that God has given us that we can adapt to any culture or context for the maximum edification of the body and the maximum glorification of Christ.

Recommended Reading

Matt Boswell, ed., *Doxology and Theology: How the Gospel Forms the Worship Leader*. Nashville. B&H Publishing, 2013.

D. A. Carson, ed., *Worship By The Book*. Grand Rapids. Zondervan, 2002.

Ligon Duncan, *Does God Care How We Worship?* Phillipsburg. P&R Publishing, 2020.

Ligon Duncan, Phil Ryken and Derek Thomas, eds., *Give Praise to God: A Vision for Reforming Worship*. Phillipsburg. P&R Publishing, 2003.

Bob Kauflin, *Worship Matters: Leading Others to Encounter the Greatness of God*. Wheaton. Crossway, 2008.

Christian Focus Publications

Our mission statement
Staying Faithful

In dependence upon God we seek to impact the world through literature faithful to His infallible Word, the Bible. Our aim is to ensure that the Lord Jesus Christ is presented as the only hope to obtain forgiveness of sin, live a useful life and look forward to heaven with Him.

Our Books are published in four imprints:

CHRISTIAN FOCUS

Popular works including biographies, commentaries, basic doctrine and Christian living.

MENTOR

Books written at a level suitable for Bible College and seminary students, pastors, and other serious readers. The imprint includes commentaries, doctrinal studies, examination of current issues and church history.

CHRISTIAN HERITAGE

Books representing some of the best material from the rich heritage of the church.

CF4KIDS

Children's books for quality Bible teaching and for all age groups: Sunday school curriculum, puzzle and activity books; personal and family devotional titles, biographies and inspirational stories – because you are never too young to know Jesus!

Christian Focus Publications Ltd,
Geanies House, Fearn, Ross-shire,
IV20 1TW, Scotland, United Kingdom.
www.christianfocus.com